To Coast Community Church

who in love and faith launched The Spirit of Elijah Ministries and in whom the seeds of this series were planted.

The Walking Worthy Series

Volume 1:
Walking Worthy As a Son of God

by Norm Wakefield

Cover Design: Josh Goforth, Goforth Graphics

ISBN: 1-892754-25-8

Contents

Introduction to the Walking Worthy Series

It is the highest of all privileges to be called by God to be His child! We have been called by His name, given the Spirit of His Son, and called to other relationships in life to express our relationship with God. The Apostle Paul wrote to the Ephesians, "Therefore I, the prisoner of the Lord, implore you to walk in a manner worthy of the *calling* with which you have been called" (Ephesians 4:1). The *calling* of which the apostle wrote was a *calling* into a relationship with God by the power of the Holy Spirit. Consequently, every aspect of a man's life will be affected.

As a man relates to God, he expresses that relationship through other *callings* in life. Biblically, a *calling* is an irrevocable act of God that establishes a special relationship with responsibilities, privileges, and promises that provide hope for the future. Paul informed the Romans that, "the gifts and the *calling* of God are irrevocable (Rom. 11:29)."

What acts of God establish a relationship that cannot be revoked? Birth establishes a relationship between parents and children, which obviously can't be changed. Marriage, according to Jesus, is an act of God, which is not to be separated by man (Mark 10:9). Since our *calling* as sons of God is irrevocable, then our relationships with brothers and sisters in Christ are established for eternity, and thus the gifts God gives by His Spirit for blessing His Body are also enduring.

Since God has called us to these earthly relationships to express our relationship with Him, it is important that we walk worthy of our *calling* as sons, husbands, fathers, and members of the body of Christ. In this series, we won't treat a man's work as a *calling* because it doesn't fit the definition as a *calling* from God. However, the responsibility to provide for his family is one of the biblical responsibilities of a man's *callings* as husband and father. Since work is such an important aspect of a man's life, an entire volume will also be devoted to how a man can walk worthy of the Lord as a provider.

Walking Worthy As a Son of God focuses our attention on our identity in Christ. You'll learn four identity principles as they relate to relationships with others and then as they pertain to your relationship with God as His son. In this first lesson, we will begin attempting to grasp and apply these identity principles.

INTRODUCTION TO WALKING WORTHY AS A SON OF GOD

Why do men do what they do? What motivates a man to work fourteen hours a day for seven days each week? Why does a husband do things at work that he wouldn't do at home? What influences a man to compromise his virginity or purity? On a positive note, why are you driving a certain kind of car? What lies behind a man's choice of the church he attends? Why do we obey God's Word?

The answers to all of these questions and many more like them are found by understanding four fundamental identity principles. A godly man needs to have a working knowledge of these principles if he is going to navigate his family through the treacherous waters of an anti-Christ culture. Overcoming sin and temptation, successfully passing on a spiritual legacy to future generations, and living a Spirit-filled life all depend on your knowing who you are. Therefore your identity in Christ must be secured and subsequently applied for you to walk worthy as a son of your Heavenly Father.

In each of the *Walking Worthy* books, you'll work with these identity principles. You will be introduced to these identity principles from two perspectives in this series. First, you will gain an understanding of each principle as you see it in the life of Christ and in the world around you. Regardless of the culture in which you live, the principles are the same although the details may be different. Second, the focus will be on how the principle is applied to your life in relationship with Jesus Christ.

Here's what you can expect in this series of lessons. Each lesson will normally have a reading assignment and life examples. Suggestions for practicing what you learn, Scripture memory, a small group interaction plan, and prayer suggestions will help make the lessons practical—encouraging you to be not only a hearer of the Word of God but also a faithful doer of His Word.

During the first lesson, you'll do the assignment and group discussion together. However, in the following lessons it will be important for you to read the brief lesson and practice the application prior to the group discussion so you will have something to share in your next group meeting. Much of what you will glean from this series will be from other men. As God works in each of your lives, you will share it with each other, take notes, and make appliation to your lives.

The goal of this series is not primarily to impart new information. The goal is to encourage the application of truth to your life, resulting in a life change for the glory of God.

LISTEN TO THE HOLY SPIRIT

As you begin this series, please pause and ask the Holy Spirit to speak to your hearts about how you might encourage one another and learn from each other as you go through this series. Write below what you hear during this time of meditation.

_____

_____

_____

_____

_____

_____

OVERVIEW OF VOLUME ONE

Volume One, *Walking Worthy As a Son of God*, focuses attention on your identity in Christ by concentrating on four identity principles. You will learn the four identity principles as they relate to relationships with others in the world, and then as they pertain to your relationship with God as His son. Each principle will be developed in two lessons making a total of eight lessons for the whole volume.

LESSON 1: IDENTITY PRINCIPLE ONE—IDENTITY HAS TO DO WITH WHOM YOU WANT TO BELONG OR CONNECT

LESSON 2: IDENTITY PRINCIPLE ONE IN CHRIST—I BELONG TO CHRIST AND HIS SPIRIT MUST FILL AND DRIVE ME SO I LIVE AS AN EXPRESSION OF THAT CONNECTION

LESSON 3: IDENTITY PRINCIPLE TWO—IDENTITY HAS TO DO WITH POWER

LESSON 4: IDENTITY PRINCIPLE TWO IN CHRIST—THE HOLY SPIRIT DWELLING WITHIN US IS OUR POWER

LESSON 5: IDENTITY PRINCIPLE THREE—THE SOURCE OF POWER SHAPES ONE'S LIFE

LESSON 6: IDENTITY PRINCIPLE THREE IN CHRIST—THE HOLY SPIRIT TRANSFORMS US INTO THE IMAGE OF JESUS CHRIST

LESSON 7: IDENTITY PRINCIPLE FOUR—FATHERS DIRECT THE IDENTITY COURSE OF THEIR CHILDREN BY WHAT THEY DO OR DON'T DO

LESSON 8: IDENTITY PRINCIPLE FOUR IN CHRIST—THE HEAVENLY FATHER DIRECTS THE IDENTITY COURSE OF HIS CHILDREN THROUGH A RELATIONSHIP WITH HIS SON, JESUS CHRIST

wants to know that we are wanted, needed, and valued by God and others. From one perspective, we're born spiritually and emotionally empty with a need to be filled. In my opinion, God provided fathers to children to be a forerunner of God's ultimate filling of that need in Himself. We'll learn more about this in the fourth principle.

WITH WHOM DO YOU WANT TO IDENTIFY?

That's the question that subconsciously drives all your choices. When a child discovers that his parents are too busy and they don't provide hope and purpose for life, then the child usually looks to his peers. For instance, let's imagine a twelve year-old boy in his Sunday School class. He notices two other boys who get the attention of the girls in his class (as well as the teacher) as they act silly, disrespectful, and flirt. Without thinking why, he reasons if he can only become friends with (belong to or connect with) those two boys, he'll be as popular as they are with the girls. So, he begins to act like them. He notices what kind of music, TV, movies, and recreation they enjoy and wants to become familiar with them so he can "relate" to the boys.

What is the typical response of parents when they notice a change of behavior in their child and an interest in things of which they do not approve? If they don't know why he's doing it, they may lecture their son about the surface issues (kinds of entertainment and choice of friends) and miss the heart of the issue—his longing to connect with someone who can offer him significance and hope which his parents haven't offered. It's a matter of identity. With whom does the child want to identify most? His parents? Or the two boys?

LIFE EXAMPLE

Karen, a sixteen year-old girl, wanted to connect with a clique in her school composed of the most popular kids in the school. Mark, a boy in the group, caught her attention. She reasoned that if she could become his girlfriend, it would elevate her social position and move her inside the important group. So she flirted with Mark, hoping to "belong" or "connect" with him. Mark finally noticed her and asked her out on a date, which was followed by other dates. Within a few weeks, Karen and Mark were a couple and identified with each other. Karen had achieved her goal of becoming popular by connecting or belonging to Mark.

Jason entered his new job at the company with fear and trembling. He didn't know anyone in the company, and his new responsibilities included

some skills he was going to have to develop. As he got to know his work
associates, he discovered the men who were the most successful had gained
favor with their boss. Jason concluded that if he could connect with those
successful men, he might advance more quickly and farther than if he didn't
connect with them. After some initial observations, Jason realized that to
belong to this group of advancing business men, he would have to work long
hours, attend weekly dinner and entertainment events, drink socially, and
develop a repertoire of crude jokes and dirty language. So that is what he did.

Can you relate to this? How would these examples be different in your
culture? Consider your elementary and early teen years. With whom did
you wish to identify, and did it not have to do with a sense of acceptance,
significance, and belonging? A particular peer group? A boyfriend or
girlfriend? A sport or athletic star? A club such as a fraternity or a sorority?
With whom are you seeking to identity now? How is this having an effect on
what you do at work? At home? At church?

PERSONAL APPLICATION

Take a few minutes and ask the Holy Spirit to show you with whom you
wished to connect when you were between the ages of 14 and 16. Note who
comes to mind. It may be a specific friend or group.

IDENTITY SOURCE

_____

_____

_____

_____

Next ask the Holy Spirit to show you with whom you wish to identify now
and the effect each is having on your life.

IDENTITY SOURCE

_____

_____

_____

_____

Each of us is a sum of the people we have met, the books we've read, the music, TV, and movies to which we've been exposed, and the impact of our culture. List some of the most influential books, movies, TV shows, or music which have contributed to your identity.

Books   Movies   Music   TV

_____   _____   _____   _____

_____   _____   _____   _____

_____   _____   _____   _____

_____   _____   _____   _____

_____   _____   _____   _____

Consider making this a topic of discussion in your family devotion time. Ask these same questions of each member of the family, and then have each one write down a list of all the people or groups to whom or which each wanted to belong.

GROUP INTERACTION

There's much to be gained from God's men growing and sharing together. As you share what is on your list, you will see that you were not the only one who experienced the reality of identity principle number one. In fact, you may be surprised how similar your experiences were and are. Share with each other what you wrote down and then write what you learned from this first lesson about your identity.

_____

_____

_____

_____

REMEMBER

The important point to remember is that **identity has to do with whom you wish to belong or connect**. There's a lot more to understand, and in the following lessons we'll build on this first principle. Until then, ask the Lord to give you and your family a deeper understanding of your own identity.

Lesson 2

IDENTITY PRINCIPLE ONE IN CHRIST

WE BELONG TO JESUS CHRIST

The memory verses at the end of this lesson state explicitly that everyone who is truly a child of God belongs to Jesus Christ. We've been given to Jesus by God, the Father. The transaction occurred when we were baptized by the Holy Spirit into Jesus. The descriptive rather than the prescriptive aspect of these verses encourages believers. They don't teach us that we are to *try* to belong to Jesus. Believers in Christ *do belong* to Jesus. Their faith and its fruit are evidences of the fact. Not only do our souls belong to Jesus, but our bodies do also. He bought us with His blood so that He might redeem us and express His life in us for His glory and that of our Father.

> *Rom. 8:9 However, you are not in the flesh but in the Spirit, if indeed the Spirit of God dwells in you. But if anyone does not have the Spirit of Christ, **he does not belong to Him**.*

The presence of the Holy Spirit in our hearts and His fruit in our lives indicate to whom we belong. Without the Spirit of Christ, no one belongs to Jesus. We can know therefore that we are identified with Jesus if we can identify the Holy Spirit within! This is how we know who is truly a Christian. Jesus warned that many people would say they are believers and know the Lord, however, not everyone who says they have accepted Jesus as their savior is truly born again. It is foundational to understand what it means to be a Christian. It's not determined by one's accepting certain facts about Jesus, joining a church, water baptism, service in the ministry, or partaking of communion, but it is by the implanting of the Life of God (the Holy Spirit) in the heart of the person. Without the presence of the Holy Spirit manifesting the life of Jesus Christ within and through the person, there is no identity in Christ and therefore no salvation.

BELIEVERS ARE CONNECTED WITH JESUS CHRIST

> *Rom. 6:5 For if we have become **united with Him** in the likeness of His death, certainly we shall also be in the likeness of His resurrection,*

> *Rom. 7:4 Therefore, my brethren, you also were made to die to the Law through the body of Christ, so that you might be **joined to another**, to Him who was raised from the dead, in order that we might bear fruit for God.*

> *1 Cor. 1:30 But by His doing **you are in Christ Jesus**, who became to us wisdom from God, and righteousness and sanctification, and redemption.*

Just as a teenager wishes to *connect* with a friend in order to be accepted in a circle of friends, so believers wish to *connect* with Jesus in order to be accepted in heaven for eternity as well as with the *Beloved* here on earth. How can two people walk in harmony together if they are not both *connected* with Jesus Christ? Paul asked the Corinthians, "What fellowship has light with darkness?" The basis of our fellowship with others is our union to, connection with, and belonging to Jesus Christ.

This connection can only be seen by our conduct, which is the fruit of the Holy Spirit's presence in our lives. If we are connected to the Holy Spirit, then we are connected with Jesus. If we are connected with Jesus, then we are connected with the eternal God and Father of creation.

Therefore, our identity with Jesus Christ is the basis of our faith, conduct, and fellowship. To what or whom are you anchored? Paul challenged the Corinthians on this point in his second letter to them. The purpose of the letter was to work out reconciliation between him and Timothy and some of the Corinthians. Repeatedly, he mentioned their common identity in Christ as the basis for their fellowship and reconciliation. In the last chapter we read this call for examination.

> *2 Cor. 13:5 Test yourselves to see if you are in the faith; examine yourselves! Or do you not recognize this about yourselves, that **Jesus Christ is in you**—unless indeed you fail the test?*

YOU SHOULD BE ABLE TO SEE JESUS CHRIST IN YOU

Paul's point: If Jesus Christ is in you, then we can fellowship together and overcome any differences or obstacles in the flesh. How is this so? Belonging and connection to Jesus Christ is the common cornerstone of everyone's identity. Since identity determines conduct, then there is a basis for an eternal relationship with God as well as with one another. A marriage cannot glorify God without both man and woman being identified with Christ. Their identity determines their attitudes, values and lifestyles. A church cannot glorify God without being cognizant of their common identity in Christ. It is their identity in Christ that distinguishes them from all other groups and organizations in society.

If you can't see Jesus in yourself and if other believers observe no spiritual fruit in your life, then you have no reason to think you belong to or are connected to Jesus Christ. You may be a "good church-goer" or a giving and helpful person for the sake of a good reputation; however, you may still be in need of the internal, eternal work of the Holy Spirit, called regeneration or new birth. If you struggle with relationships with other believers, there may be reason to take Paul's test given to the Corinthians. If you fail the test, consider how blessed you are to know where you stand while you are still breathing! There's time to turn from identifying with the world and its values and to turn to Jesus Christ. Just as Paul expressed his goal to the Galatians, you should not be satisfied until Jesus Christ is formed in you (4:19)—until you see the evidence that you belong to and are connected with Jesus Christ.

If you have seen Jesus Christ living in you on a regular basis, then you have great cause to rejoice and build relationships with others who are in Christ! When relationships get difficult, set your mind on the fact of who you are and who they are in Christ. Then conduct yourself and speak according to the truth, and you will bring glory to God and walk in peace with God and man.

LIFE EXAMPLE

Jessica felt trapped and hopeless. Her two children were clearly identifying with their peers at school and the godless culture around them. She could tell their hearts were gone. Disrespect, thoughtlessness, and rejection characterized their relationship with her. How could she expect otherwise? She worked from 8:00 a.m. to 5:00 p.m. five days a week and spent three evenings each week in church activities. They passed each other like ships in the night with hardly a wave or acknowledgement of relationship. She had thought years ago that being a career woman and an active women's leader in her church was what her parents, husband, and church friends expected. In wanting to be identified with them and to be accepted, she had pursued that course with all her energies and was successful. But now she felt trapped.

Her children needed her! They were becoming a shame to her. As she prayed for her children, she knew they needed more time from her and their father. Jessica desperately wanted to prevent the destruction that was imminent. But how could anything change? To do what she needed to do would mean a drastic change in her identity and lifestyle. If she wanted to connect with her children and do what she knew the Bible revealed she was to do as a mother, she would have to choose between what her church and culture expected of her and what God required of her.

In her search for answers, Jessica attended a homeschool conference. As she listened, she realized she had elevated her identity as a career woman and women's minister above her identity in Christ and as a wife and mother. It had cost her dearly, and her husband and children even more. God's Word said she was to be her husband's helpmeet, but she had been much more successful as her employer's helpmeet. God's Word revealed she was to love and train her children, but she had viewed them as hindrances.

In her heart, she knew the first step was an issue of identity. She would repent of seeking to identify with her parents, church friends, and culture and live consistent with her identity in Christ. She belonged to Him and therefore His words and approval were of most importance. As she made that decision, she experienced a wonderful release. She was no longer trapped by her old identity. She was a new creature and she would act like one. This set her free to resign her job and dedicate her heart and energies to her family. The change brought about remarkable changes in the children when she began teaching them at home.

Jessica's identity as a career woman and church leader had been motivated by a desire to be accepted and have something in common with her peer group and parents. She belonged to them and desired to be connected. She was living as if her only identity was as a member of those groups of people. Consequently, her life didn't have the blessing of God because what her peers expected was not what God's Word revealed was His design for a wife and mother. As she heard what God's Word required of her, she realized she would have to choose with whom she wanted to identify most: her church, culture, and parents or Jesus Christ. As a believer, she realized she really had no choice! She belonged to Him and thus, He had the place of authority in her life. Having settled her identity, she was free to do what she knew was best for her husband and children.

Bill's story also demonstrates the importance of identity in Jesus Christ. Before being born again by the Spirit of God, his identity was rooted primarily in gaining the approval of his own pride and peers.

For the first twenty-nine years of his life, Bill's identity was sports, his wife, and ministry in the church. He thought (because he had been told) he was a Christian because he had invited Jesus into his heart when he was twelve. For seventeen years, he sought to find significance in life through achievement. This desire to achieve and be significant, along with his natural gifts and abilities led him into the youth ministry.

By the time he was twenty-five, Bill began to experience tremendous guilt and frustration because of his powerlessness to overcome impurity, lust, and his inability to love his wife and family. He worked from early in the morning until late at night and had little time for his wife and children, which took a heavy toll on their relationships. Bill didn't understand what the problem was. He was unhappy, overwhelmed with ministry responsibilities (the ministry was growing and seemingly successful), his wife was unfulfilled, his children were out of control, and he felt guilty and distant from God.

After four years, his conscience would not allow him to maintain the charade of being a minister to others in Jesus' name when his private life was so fruitless. So he resigned his ministry position to pursue attending a denominational seminary, mistakenly concluding he needed more Bible information. He was still identifying with the church and ministry as his source of significance.

God graciously prevented him from seeking more theological knowledge as an answer to Bill's problems. God saw his identity in ministry and pursuit of knowledge as an idol in his heart rooted in pride. Bill met some men who knew that the presence of the Holy Spirit and the new birth were what was needed in his life. They became spiritual fathers to him and began leading him to encounter Jesus personally. He became thirsty and hungry to experience the life of Christ more than achievement in work and ministry. How could he minister in power and love to his family and others without his identity being firmly anchored in Jesus Christ, Himself? He realized he couldn't, and thus began to seek with all his heart to connect with Jesus.

Bill was born again. He repented of his pride and worship of self-achievement and rejoiced that his sin had been removed at the cross by his union with Jesus Christ. Finally, he knew by faith that he belonged to the heavenly Father and was connected eternally to Christ. The presence and ministry of Jesus was evident in his heart as the Holy Spirit cleansed his conscience, turned his heart toward God, his wife, and children, and filled him with peace. Changes took place in his life also. Self-ambition and achievement in ministry were no longer idols. He didn't feel compelled to let the demands of ministry control his life because he realized it wasn't *his* identity and ministry, but it was *God's* ministry. This liberated him to love his wife, lead his family, and return to ministry in the power of the Holy Spirit.

YOU CAN'T HAVE TWO MASTERS

In these examples perhaps you can see that the conflicts Jessica and Bill had were identity conflicts. They found they had to make a choice between two masters. They couldn't identify with both the values and expectations of their culture and identify with Jesus Christ. Jesus taught in the Sermon on the Mount that a man cannot have two masters. "For either he will hate the one and love the other, or he will be devoted to one and despise the other" (Matthew 6:24). Jessica and Bill experienced that truth. And so will you.

Jesus' call to discipleship and salvation is a call to a new identity. Read carefully the following verses.

> *Luke 14:26 If anyone comes to Me, and does not hate his own father and mother and wife and children and brothers and sisters, yes, and even his own life, he cannot be My disciple.*

> *Luke 14:27 Whoever does not carry his own cross and come after Me cannot be My disciple.*

> *Luke 14:33 So then, none of you can be My disciple who does not give up all his own possessions.*

Jesus wasn't telling them to *actually* hate their family members and give up every single possession. Other Scriptures clearly tell us to love our spouses and children and to be good stewards of what God gives us. So what was He saying? Jesus was saying this: to be a disciple of His and to be saved, one must identify more with Jesus than with his culture, self-comfort, or materialism. A man can only have one master, one identity—Jesus Christ.

TO WHOM DO YOU BELONG?

The truth is that we will act according to whom we belong or identify. We might *say* we belong to Christ, but our actions reveal what is really on the inside of the heart. The following exercises are purposefully designed to help you grasp the reality of who you and the members of your family are identified with. You may be identifying more with your culture or peers than Jesus without realizing it—while testifying that you are Christian. As you have read this assignment, write down your thoughts or questions below.

_____

_____

_____

_____

Before you attend your small group meeting, lead your family in the following exercises. Take notes of what was shared so you can share it with the group.

PERSONAL APPLICATION

In order to stimulate some discussion on this idea of identification with Christ, you might ask some of the following questions:

1.   How can we tell if someone is identified with a particular political party in their nation?

_____

_____

2.   What would we expect to happen if we put a mouse into cage with three hungry cats? Why?

_____

_____

3.   What would we expect to happen if a non-believer married a believer in Jesus Christ? Why?

_____

_____

_____

4.   What would we expect to happen in a church if there were unbelieving churchmembers? Why?

_____

_____

_____

5. Read the following verses and write down the characteristics of someone who is identified with Jesus Christ and has His Spirit living within them. (You may want to do one each day or do them all at once.)

Matt. 7:15-24

_____

_____

1 John 3:3-10

_____

_____

1 John 4:1-8, 20

_____

_____

Romans 8:9-16

_____

_____

James 4:4-5

_____

_____

*2 Cor. 13:5 Test yourselves to see if you are in the faith; examine yourselves! Or do you not recognize this about yourselves, that **Jesus Christ is in you**—unless indeed you fail the test?*

PERSONAL PRAYER INVITATION

What have you learned about yourself in this lesson? Ask the Holy Spirit to speak to your heart. Ask Him what He sees in light of the verses in this lesson. Write down what comes to mind.

_____

_____

_____

_____

Interact with Jesus on a personal level. What should you say to Him in response to what came to your mind? If you are a believer in Jesus will you live your life as a demonstration of that connection? Each morning, I encourage you to remind yourself of who you are in Christ.

- I belong to Jesus.

- His Spirit lives within me and is my source of power.

- His Spirit will change me as He fills and lives in me.

- I am blessed to be God's son.

- I will consider my old self as having died and will be alive to what the life of God in me loves and hates.

- Father, please give me the fullness of the Holy Spirit as you promised through Jesus Christ for your glory.

May the Lord work in your life as you renew your minds as to your identification with Jesus Christ. Hopefully you are prepared now to be an encouragement and blessing to the small group as you share what you have experienced with Jesus Christ and your family.

SCRIPTURE MEMORY

Choose two or more verses to memorize this week.

Romans 6:5 For if we have become **united with Him** in the likeness of His death, certainly we shall also be in the likeness of His resurrection...

Rom. 7:4 Therefore, my brethren, you also were made to die to the Law through the body of Christ, so that you might be *joined to another, to Him who was raised from the dead, in order that we might bear fruit for God.*

*1 Cor. 1:30 But by His doing **you are in Christ Jesus**, who became to us wisdom from God, and righteousness and sanctification, and redemption.*

*1 Cor. 3:23 And you **belong to Christ**; and Christ belongs to God.*

*1 Cor. 6:19 Or do you not know that your body is a temple of the Holy Spirit who is in you, whom you have from God, and that you are **not your own?***

*2 Cor. 13:5 Test yourselves to see if you are in the faith; examine yourselves! Or do you not recognize this about yourselves, that **Jesus Christ is in you**—unless indeed you fail the test?*

*Gal. 3:29 And if you **belong to Christ**, then you are Abraham's descendants, heirs according to promise.*

*Gal. 5:24 Now those who **belong to Christ Jesus** have crucified the flesh with its passions and desires.*

*Rom. 8:9 However, you are not in the flesh but in the Spirit, if indeed the Spirit of God dwells in you. But if anyone does not have the Spirit of Christ, **he does not belong to Him**.*

GROUP INTERACTION

1. Begin with prayer, acknowledging the identity truths you've been declaring each morning.

2. Each member of the group quote the two verses he memorized and share what was meaningful about them.

3. Share what thoughts or questions you had after reading the assignment.

4. Share about your personal application exercises.

5. Read the list of verses from Lesson Two, exercise 5, and make a list of the biblical characteristics of those who are identified with Christ.

6. Share what you experienced as you began each day declaring your identity in Christ.

7. Close with prayer for one another and for God's guidance as you study Lesson 3.

Lesson 3

IDENTITY PRINCIPLE TWO

It is important to know and understand identity principles because they equip you with tools to understand yourself, your spouse, your children, and why you do what you do (or don't do what you don't do). Your identity determines how you respond to people and situations, why you develop the relationships you develop, and what values you have. When a child's identity is secure, he or she has a built-in protection from the world's destructive appeals. The primary goal of this series is to secure your identity in Jesus Christ and to help you know what it means to walk by the Holy Spirit. Knowing with certainty that you belong to and are connected with Jesus Christ is foundational to living consistently filled with the Holy Spirit.

In the first lesson, you made a list of people with whom you wanted to connect with as a teenager and as an adult. Why is it that you wanted to connect with them? The answer reveals the second identity principle.

IDENTITY PRINCIPLE TWO: IDENTITY HAS TO DO WITH POWER

Before we look at this principle in life, let's notice the relationship of identity and power revealed in an encounter between Simon Peter and Jesus. In Matthew 16, Jesus talked with Simon Peter about this issue of identity. Jesus asked Simon who he thought He was. Simon replied that he believed Jesus was the Son of the living God, the Messiah. On the basis of Simon's response, Jesus gave Simon a new name (identity), Peter, meaning *Rock*. He also informed Peter that this revelation of Jesus' identity was an indication not of natural intellect or understanding, but of revelation from Jesus' father! We might say that Jesus was informing Peter that he was now *connected to* or *belonged to* His father in heaven.

This new connection was a *powerful* connection. In fact, Jesus said, it was how His church was going to be built—the powerful connection between His heavenly father and the members of His church. This power comes through the revelation regarding Jesus' identity. It's a power that even the gates of hell cannot withstand. Jesus told Peter:

> *I also say to you that you are Peter, and upon this rock I will build My church; and the gates of Hades will not overpower it. I will give you the keys of the kingdom of heaven; and whatever you bind on earth shall have been bound in heaven, and whatever you loose on earth shall have been loosed in heaven (Matthew 16:18-19).*

It is helpful for our understanding to see that Jesus' connection and belonging to His father was the source of His power. After being tempted by the devil, we read, "And Jesus returned to Galilee in the **power of the Spirit**" (Luke 4:14). Where did that power come from? From His father! Jesus was recorded by the Apostle John, "**My Father is working** until now, and I Myself am working" (John 5:17). Jesus didn't do anything on His own initiative, but drew His words and strength from His father. "Do you not believe that I am in the Father, and the Father is in Me? The words that I say to you I do not speak on My own initiative, **but the Father abiding in Me does His works**" (John 14:10). Jesus' display of power testifies to His identity as the Son of the living God.

What do our actions display? They testify to our source(s) of identity. You don't want to connect with someone unless he offers you something you treasure or hope for. This is human nature. It is the power to fill or to provide significance or a perceived happiness that attracts you. The reason you want to be identified with a person, group, or organization is the perceived gain you think is associated.

For instance, in the first lesson, we read about Karen, who pursued a friendship (a connection) with a popular, good-looking boy because with that association came popularity, significance, or the power to influence people. Another example: a fatherless, inner-city youth joins a gang because he thinks it opens the door for him to girls, money, and influence (power). In a sense, the gang also becomes a surrogate father and family, making him feel significant. Each fall, on many college campuses, the fraternities and sororities seek to lure incoming freshmen into their clubs. Each organization seeks to convince the freshmen of the advantages of being associated with them. The students will join the fraternity or sorority he or she thinks will provide the most benefit. Identity is about power.

LIFE EXAMPLE

Matt was sixteen and insecure about the way he looked, so when he first met Sue, a beautiful and gifted pastor's daughter, he was attracted to her. If he was associated with Sue, the rest of the guys would really think he was something. He had to be to get a beautiful girl like Sue to be with him! He realized also that his social status would increase with her by his side. If she belonged to him and he to her, he wouldn't feel so insecure and insignificant. She offered him the power of significance, acceptance, and self-assurance.

Stephen was overcome with guilt because of hidden private sin. His relationship with his wife was suffering because of it and spiritually he was empty. However, Stephen was quite successful in business and had significant financial resources. In an effort to deal with his inadequacies and guilt, he decided to build a relationship with the senior pastor of his church. He first got the attention of his pastor with very generous contributions to the church and then began to take the pastor to dinner on a regular basis. As the relationship grew, Stephen didn't feel quite so guilty about his sin and didn't realize he was still spiritually empty. He had filled the void with a relationship with someone who he thought was what he wanted to be like. Therefore he felt that he was achieving some spiritual growth and significance. Stephen became a deacon in his church and was honored because he was associated with the senior pastor. What power did the pastor offer to Stephen? As a result of the relationship, Stephen received social acceptance, significance, and personal affirmation.

Cathy was an exceptional student and was excited about pursuing a career as a journalist. As she considered where she would attend college, at the top of the list was a college she knew was recognized by the major news and magazine outlets in the United States. She knew if she had a degree from that institution, her market value would be far above graduates from other schools. Clearly Cathy's choice was wise because of the benefit to her career plans.

Each of these life examples reveals Identity Principle Two: Identity has to do with power. You connect with people or belong to organizations because they provide something you need or desire. The following exercises are purposefully designed to help you grasp *why* you and the members of your family are identified with certain people, organizations, and ultimately Jesus Christ. Before doing the family identity exercises, write down your thoughts or questions below as a result of reading this lesson.

_____

_____

_____

_____

Before you attend your small group meeting, lead your family in the following exercises. Take notes of what was shared so you can share it with the group.

PERSONAL APPLICATION

1. In the first lesson, you made a list of the people and groups with whom you wanted to connect when you were between the ages of 14-16 and now as an adult. Now take those same names and ask yourself, "What did I think I would gain if I connected with that person?" What did you stand to gain by knowing and connecting with them? Write your answer in the right column below. After you have done this exercise, lead your family to do the same.

IDENTITY SOURCE (14-16)   POWER THEY OFFERED

_____   _____

_____   _____

_____   _____

_____   _____

_____   _____

IDENTITY SOURCE (NOW)   POWER THEY OFFERED

_____   _____

_____   _____

_____   _____

_____   _____

2. It is also helpful to look at this principle from another angle. There are people in your life who have sought to be associated or identified with you because you are a blessing to them. Below, note the names of people in your life who are connected with you in the left column and the blessing you are to them in the right column.

IDENTIFYING WITH YOU   **POWER YOU OFFER**

_____   _____

_____   _____

_____   _____

_____   _____

_____   _____

_____   _____

PERSONAL PRAYER INVITATION

What have you learned about yourself in this lesson? Ask the Holy Spirit to speak to your heart. Ask Him what He sees in light of the verses in this lesson. Write down what comes to mind.

_____

_____

_____

_____

Interact with Jesus on a personal level. When you look to someone instead of God as your source of identity, He considers that idol worship. If you have turned from trusting in those relationships and what they offer and have turned to trust in God through Jesus Christ, then you have much for which to give thanks! Have you ever expressed your repentance and sorrow for having sought power from another source than God? Thank Him for being your source of power and for revealing Himself to you. Again this week, as soon as you are aware of being awake, I encourage you to remind yourself of who you are in Christ. If you memorize this, you'll be able to renew your mind more effectively as to your identity in Christ.

• I belong to Jesus.

- His Spirit lives within me and is my source of power.

- His Spirit will change me as He fills and lives in me.

- I am blessed to be God's son.

- I will consider my old self as having died and will be alive to what the life of God in me loves and hates.

- Father, please give me the fullness of the Holy Spirit as you promised through Jesus Christ for your glory.

SCRIPTURE MEMORY

Choose two or more scriptures to memorize this week.

> *Matthew 16:18-19 I also say to you that you are Peter, and upon this rock I will build My church; and the gates of Hades will not overpower it. I will give you the keys of the kingdom of heaven; and whatever you bind on earth shall have been bound in heaven, and whatever you loose on earth shall have been loosed in heaven.*

> *Jeremiah 32:17 Ah Lord GOD! Behold, You have made the heavens and the earth by Your great power and by Your outstretched arm! Nothing is too difficult for You.*

> *Ezekiel 24:21 Speak to the house of Israel, "Thus says the Lord GOD, 'Behold, I am about to profane My sanctuary, the pride of your power, the desire of your eyes and the delight of your soul; and your sons and your daughters whom you have left behind will fall by the sword.'"*

> *2 Chronicles 16:9 "For the eyes of the LORD move to and fro throughout the earth that He may strongly support those whose heart is completely His. You have acted foolishly in this. Indeed, from now on you will surely have wars."*

GROUP INTERACTION

1. Begin with prayer, acknowledging the identity truths you've been declaring each morning and the power God offers to you as you meet.

2. Each member of the group quote the two verses he memorized and share what was meaningful about them.

3. Share what thoughts or questions you had after reading the assignment.

4. Share about your personal application on Identity Principle Two.

5. Discuss what power you are receiving by belonging to this small group.

6. Share what you experienced as you began each day declaring your identity in Christ.

7. Close with prayer for one another and for God's guidance as you study Lesson 4.

Lesson 4

IDENTITY PRINCIPLE TWO IN CHRIST

When you are facing responsibilities, do you rely on your own strength? It's easy to do. We do it without thinking—without thinking about who we belong to. We belong to and are connected to our heavenly Father through our faith in Jesus Christ, His Son. One of the astounding blessings of salvation is a new relationship with God. We see with the eyes of faith that the Father of Jesus Christ has become our Father!

The Apostle Paul wrote to the Galatians, "Because you are sons, God has sent forth the Spirit of His Son into our hearts, crying, "Abba! Father!" (4:7). This great truth unveils the second identity principle: Identity has to do with power. As believers in Christ, we have become connected to the greatest power source known to mankind. He is available all the time and in any circumstance. Let's look at what God's Word reveals about the Holy Spirit and His relationship to power in our lives.

IDENTITY PRINCIPLE TWO: IDENTITY HAS TO DO WITH POWER—THE HOLY SPIRIT DWELLING WITHIN US IS OUR POWER FROM GOD

The following verses attest to the source of power dwelling in Jesus–it was the Holy Spirit. Jesus' life could not be explained apart from the indwelling and ministry of the Spirit of God.

*Luke 1:35 The angel answered and said to her, "The Holy Spirit will come upon you, and the **power** of the Most High will overshadow you; and for that reason the holy Child shall be called the Son of God."*

*Luke 4:14 And Jesus returned to Galilee in the **power** of the Spirit, and news about Him spread through all the surrounding district.*

THE HOLY SPIRIT'S PRESENCE CONFIRMS JESUS HAS BEEN GLORIFIED

What an indescribable gift we have been given by the Father and the Son! Because we are sons/daughters of God, He has given us His Spirit to fill us and empower us. Let the truth and the abundance of these verses thrill your soul. We know Jesus has been glorified before the Father because the Holy Spirit lives in us.

John 7:38-39 "He who believes in Me, as the Scripture said, 'From his innermost being will flow rivers of living water.'" But this He spoke of the Spirit, whom those who believed in Him were to receive; for the Spirit was not yet given, because Jesus was not yet glorified.

The power of the Holy Spirit has been given and is available to every believer. It is our birthright.

The power of the Holy Spirit is primarily for holy living and thus, powerful witnessing. It is the Holy Spirit who manifests the life of Jesus Christ—His presence—in the lives of God's children. He gives us gifts for ministry to others as a means of building up the body into the full image of Jesus Christ.

Believers, however, must be discerning when it comes to the gifts of the Holy Spirit because there are counterfeit spirits who will produce destructive results in the lives of the unsuspecting and undiscerning. God's Word clearly teaches that gifts are not for show, but for ministry to the body of Christ and that signs and wonders were also acts of ministry and deliverance.

1 Cor. 12:4-7 Now there are varieties of gifts, but the same Spirit. And there are varieties of ministries, and the same Lord. There are varieties of effects, but the same God who works all things in all persons. But to each one is given the manifestation of the Spirit for the common good.

1 Cor. 14:26 What is the outcome then, brethren? When you assemble, each one has a psalm, has a teaching, has a revelation, has a tongue, has an interpretation. Let all things be done for edification.

Therefore, ecstatic experiences such as speaking in tongues without interpretation, slaying in the spirit, barking like dogs, or "holy" laughter are exposed for what they really are: the manifestation of spirits other than the Holy Spirit. None of these manifestations are affirmed in the Scriptures and thus should be suspected. God's Word is our rule for faith and practice. These counterfeit experiences are powerful, but their source is a dark power masquerading as light. Their presence judges God's children to see if they will live by God's Word for His glory or by their experiences. Often people who are not born again by God's Spirit open themselves to these experiences and are led to think they are Christians because they can speak in tongues or have been "slain in the Spirit" by a "prophet". Others gain an attitude of spiritual superiority and pride because they have received the "blessing."

The fruit of the Holy Spirit's ministry is clearly stated in Scripture. In all of the Apostle Paul's writing, the ministry of the Holy Spirit leads believers to put to death the flesh-life and to put on the life of Jesus Christ (Gal. 5:16-17, Rom. 8:12-16). This is the direction of the power from above. Notice the power available to believers in the following verses.

*Luke 24:49 "And behold, I am sending forth the promise of My Father upon you; but you are to stay in the city until you are clothed with **power** from on high."*

*Acts: 1:8 But you will receive **power** when the Holy Spirit has come upon you; and you shall be My witnesses both in Jerusalem, and in all Judea and Samaria, and even to the remotest part of the earth.*

*Rom. 15:13 Now may the God of hope fill you with all joy and peace in believing, so that you will abound in hope by the **power** of the Holy Spirit.*

*1 Cor. 4:20 For the kingdom of God does not consist in words but in **power**.*

*2 Cor. 4:7 But we have this treasure in earthen vessels, so that the surpassing greatness of the **power** will be of God and not from ourselves...*

*Eph. 1:19 [may the eyes of your hearts be enlightened to see] what is the surpassing greatness of His **power** toward us who believe. These are in accordance with the working of the strength of His might*

*Eph. 3:16 that He would grant you, according to the riches of His glory, to be strengthened with **power** through His Spirit in the inner man...*

*Phil. 3:10 that I may know Him and the **power** of His resurrection and the fellowship of His sufferings, being conformed to His death;*

*Col. 1:11 [I pray that you be] strengthened with all **power**, according to His glorious might, for the attaining of all steadfastness and patience; joyously*

*2 Tim. 1:7 For God has not given us a spirit of timidity, but of **power** and love and discipline.*

*1 Pet. 1:5 who are protected by the **power** of God through faith for a salvation ready to be revealed in the last time.*

*2 Pet. 1:3 seeing that His divine **power** has granted to us everything pertaining to life and godliness, through the true knowledge of Him who called us by His own glory and excellence.*

*Eph. 3:20 Now to Him who is able to do far more abundantly beyond all that we ask or think, according to the **power** that works within us.*

Have you ever felt like you didn't have the strength to do what God requires? Sure you have! All of us have. We don't have the strength without a conscious reliance and relationship with Jesus through the power of the Holy Spirit. How are we to love our children? How are they to love us? How can a husband and wife be faithful and love one another? How can children obey their parents? How can we obey our Lord? The answer to all of these questions is the same: Only by the power of the Holy Spirit. That's why He was given to us!

The verses above inform us of the riches that are ours because we belong to the Father and the Lord Jesus Christ. If you belong to Christ, then you have His Spirit. If you don't have His Spirit then you don't belong to Christ.

Rom. 8:9 However, you are not in the flesh but in the Spirit, if indeed the Spirit of God dwells in you. But if anyone does not have the Spirit of Christ, he does not belong to Him.

WHY BE CONNECTED TO JESUS?

As we studied the previous lesson, we discovered the reason a person wishes to connect or belong to another person is that he obtains something he values from that association. A teen befriends another teen because he or she thinks they can increase popularity or gain certain social or financial advantages. It's about power. The same is true about our relationship with God through Jesus Christ—it's about power. Why should you or anyone seek a relationship with Jesus Christ? Because He is the only way to the Father! Because He has publicly and historically demonstrated the power to defeat death, sin, and Satan! Because we are sinners and His death and resurrection set us free from sin's penalty, power, and ultimately, its presence! Because the Father and the Son have *promised* the Holy Spirit to those who believe in and daily apply what

Jesus has done and promised.

The Holy Spirit, who empowered the Son of God, Jesus, is the only way anyone can live to glorify God as they fulfill their daily responsibilities to love, serve, and be light. You need Him. Your children need Him. Without Him, you cannot experience fullness in life. Have you been content to live without the fullness of the Holy Spirit? Have you tried to train, teach, and love your children without being filled with the Rivers of Living Water? Have you and your family members been careless in their relationship with the Holy Spirit?

This lesson has focused on Identity Principle Two in Christ: Identity has to do with power. You connect to Jesus because He provides everything you need. The following exercises are purposefully designed to help you grow in your identity with Jesus Christ. Take a moment to jot down your thoughts or questions below as a result of reading this lesson.

_____

_____

_____

_____

Before you attend your small group meeting, lead your family in the following exercises. Take notes of what was shared so you can share it with the group.

PERSONAL APPLICATION

1. How is it with you and the Holy Spirit? This week I recommend a Holy Spirit relationship check. After reading through the verses above, take some time to consider your relationship with the Holy Spirit. He is the presence of Christ in your life. Have you grieved or quenched Him in any way? Read Ephesians 4:25-5:33, and as a family, make a list of what grieves and encourages the presence and fullness of the Holy Spirit.

_____

_____

_____

_____

2. What do you think one will experience if he or she has been careless, grieved the Holy Spirit, not repented, or made the relationship right? What

might one expect from the Holy Spirit if he or she valued a relationship with the Holy Spirit and kept the relationship free from grievances?

_____

_____

_____

_____

PERSONAL PRAYER INVITATION

What have you learned about the Holy Spirit and yourself in this lesson? Ask the Holy Spirit to speak to your heart. You need the Holy Spirit to guide you as you pray. Listen to Him as He tells you where and when you have grieved Him. Write down what comes to mind. Express your heart to Him honestly and often. If you belong to Christ, walk in and with His Spirit—He is your power source!

_____

_____

_____

_____

Please continue to practice your morning confession of identity. Remember:

- I belong to Jesus.

- His Spirit lives within me and is my source of power.

- His Spirit will change me as He fills and lives in me.

- I am blessed to be God's son.

- I will consider my old self as having died and will be alive to what the life of God in me loves and hates.

- Father, please give me the fullness of the Holy Spirit as you promised through Jesus Christ for your glory.

SCRIPTURE MEMORY

Choose two or more scriptures to memorize this week.

Romans 15:13 _Now may the God of hope fill you with all joy and_ *peace in believing, so that you will abound in hope by the **power** of the Holy Spirit.*

*1 Cor. 4:20 For the kingdom of God does not consist in words but in **power.***

*2 Cor. 4:7 But we have this treasure in earthen vessels, so that the surpassing greatness of the **power** will be of God and not from ourselves;*

*Eph. 1:19 ...[may the eyes of your hearts be enlightened to see] what is the surpassing greatness of His **power** toward us who believe. These are in accordance with the working of the strength of His might.*

*Eph. 3:16 ...that He would grant you, according to the riches of His glory, to be strengthened with **power** through His Spirit in the inner man...*

*Eph. 3:20 Now to Him who is able to do far more abundantly beyond all that we ask or think, according to the **power** that works within us...*

*Philippians 3:10 ...that I may know Him and the **power** of His resurrection and the fellowship of His sufferings, being conformed to His death...*

*Colossians 1:11 [I pray that you be] strengthened with all **power**, according to His glorious might, for the attaining of all steadfastness and patience; joyously...*

*2 Timothy 1:7 For God has not given us a spirit of timidity, but of **power** and love and discipline.*

*1 Peter 1:5 ...who are protected by the **power** of God through faith for a salvation ready to be revealed in the last time.*

*2 Peter 1:3 ...seeing that His divine **power** has granted to us everything pertaining to life and godliness, through the true knowledge of Him who called us by His own glory and excellence.*

GROUP INTERACTION

1. Begin with prayer, acknowledging the identity truths you've been declaring each morning. Also thank the Holy Spirit for His presence and power.

2. Each member of the group quote the two verses he memorized and share

what was meaningful about them.

3. Share what thoughts or questions you had after reading the assignment.

4. Share about your personal application exercises.

5. Confess to the group the ways you have grieved the Holy Spirit and then pray for each other. James 5:16 encourages you to, "Confess your sins to one another, and pray for one another so that you may be healed. The effective prayer of a righteous man can accomplish much."

6. Share what you experienced as you began each day declaring your identity in Christ and repenting for grieving the Holy Spirit.

7. Close with prayer for one another and for God's guidance as you study Lesson 5.

Lesson 5

IDENTITY PRINCIPLE THREE

The last two weeks we discussed the fact that when we wish to connect with or identify with someone, we do so because we believe there is something to be gained from the association. They have a power we don't have, and subconsciously (or perhaps consciously) we deduce that we can have that power if we are connected to them. Once we conclude there's something to be gained, we begin to look for ways to connect with them.

IDENTITY PRINCIPLE THREE: THE SOURCE OF IDENTITY SHAPES YOUR LIFE

We've been studying the passage in Matthew 16 when Jesus and Simon Peter were discussing identity. Jesus had asked His disciples who they considered Him to be. Simon responded, "You're the Christ, the Son of the living God." Surely Jesus' reply astounded Simon. "Blessed are you, Simon Barjona, because flesh and blood did not reveal this to you, but My Father who is in heaven. I also say to you that you are Peter, and upon this rock I will build My church; and the gates of Hades will not overpower it" (17-18). Not only was Jesus implying that Peter belonged to *His* father, but also that His father was going to shape his life. Furthermore, the entire church, the true church of Christ, would be shaped by the power of His father's revealing work.

Like Christ, it should be obvious to others who our father is: the living God. When we read the gospels, we can't help but notice who controlled Jesus' life: the word and will of His father. Jesus' source of identity was the living God. He declared more than once that He and the Father were identified with each other (John 10:30; John 14:9). Jesus never spoke on His own initiative (John

12:49; 14:10; 16:13) nor acted without perfect conformity to the will of His father (John 5:30; 8:28). Jesus' life here on earth was entirely shaped by the life of His father because He was the source of identity and power for the Son.

During those heated conversations between Jesus and the Pharisees, Jesus used this third principle of identity. Who shaped the lives of the Pharisees? Their father, the Devil! Because they were identified with him and he was their source of power, they could not and would not identify with Jesus and His father. Jesus understood the root of their actions and words—*the source of their identity*.

When it comes to life, we are all shaped by those with whom we wish to identify. Here's how it happens. In an effort to gain some personal benefit that we think will fill us, we desire to connect with a person or group. However, perhaps without realizing it, we go through a process of transformation. The next thing we do is find out what is required of us to make the connection by observing the individual or learning the expectations of the leaders of the group. Then we either imitate those with whom we wish to identify or we change our actions and words to gain their approval based on *their* values.

There is an alternate identity dynamic that shapes our lives that may take place. Some people have such bitterness toward an individual or group that in reaction, they determine they will do nothing that closely identifies them with that individual or group. They don't want anyone to think they are associated; therefore without realizing it, their lives are being shaped by someone with whom they are offended or embittered.

In either example above, their lives are being shaped by this third identity principle being worked out in their lives. Let's look at some examples.

LIFE EXAMPLE

A deacon and his wife were troubled about their son, **Eric**, age 12. Recently, he had displayed attitudes of disrespect and unusual, almost addictive, interest in a particular electronic game. They discovered Eric's obsession one evening when they knocked to enter his bedroom and the door was locked. Eric opened the door after repeated demands. His loving, concerned parents sought explanation for why the door was locked. After a few lame excuses and hemming and hawing around, Eric finally revealed the cause: he was engrossed in an electronic game of which he knew they wouldn't approve.

This event prompted an important discussion about their relationship and recent events in Eric's life. What had happened in his life that fostered the recent deterioration in respect? Where did he get the game? Why didn't he ask them about the game? Had they done something to damage their relationship? Did Eric think God was pleased with the game that involved immodestly dressed characters and violence?

For Eric, becoming good at the popular electronic game was his avenue to connect with the most popular kid in his class, Jerry, as well as all of Jerry's friends. It wasn't the only way he tried to fit in with Jerry's world. He adopted Jerry's attitude toward authority (thus the disrespect to parents), began using crude and filthy language, developed an appetite for pornography, acquired new clothing styles, and imitated a host of other qualities and activities he had observed in Jerry—EVEN THOUGH HE KNEW THEY WERE WRONG. The deacon and his wife had only seen the tip of the iceberg that evening when they happened upon Eric's locked bedroom door.

The problem Eric and his parents were facing illustrates the third identity principle that combines the first two principles. Once we pick a source with which or whom to identity, we let it shape our lives! Other illustrations come to mind. Consider the affect of the military, gangs, fraternities and sororities, or a boyfriend or girlfriend. Do you remember when you first thought your husband or wife was someone to whom you wished to be connected? What a power they held over your life!

If Eric's parents understood these first three principles, they would know why he was doing what he was doing—Eric was trying to identify with someone at school. Bedrooms of teens can be quite revealing! The pictures on the walls, the CD's and DVD's on the shelves, and the clothes in the closet can tell a story. It doesn't take a rocket scientist to deduce with whom or what the teen is identifying. Their lives reveal it. The same is true for adults!

Boomer (not his real name) was a relatively new addition to a fellowship that had been studying these identity principles. One Sunday morning, in walked Boomer *without* his trademark ponytail. The pastor had never known him without it, and he was shocked by Boomer's neatly trimmed haircut. Out of belief that changes like that need to be led by the Holy Spirit and not social pressure, the minister questioned him as to why he cut his hair. The pastor was hoping it wasn't because someone had put a guilt trip on him with a goal to get him to conform to a self-righteous standard.

Boomer told the pastor the Holy Spirit had applied the first three identity principles to his life. He had never realized that the reason he had long hair in the first place was because he wished to identify with the rebellion of the 70's. Boomer told the pastor how he had grown long hair as a statement that he wasn't a part of the old establishment. As he grew older, matured, and came to Christ, he had separated from the rebellious youth culture. In fact, he was ashamed of it! During the previous meeting, the Holy Spirit had revealed to him that his long hair was a matter of rebellious pride. He grew it long in order to connect with a sub-culture with which he no longer wished to be identified. Boomer knew in his heart God was asking him to cut his hair as a testimony he belonged to Him. Although he had worn his hair long for 20 years, he wanted to do it! Boomer had already settled the issue that his life was going to be shaped by his relationship with Jesus Christ. He just hadn't made the connection yet in this area of his life.

By the way, for those of you who have long hair, I'm not suggesting from this illustration that all men having long hair are rebellious and proud. I'm merely giving an example of how this third principle may be used to produce sanctification and a greater identity with Jesus Christ. For Boomer, one application was his hair length. For you and your children it may be something else. The questions are these:

1. Why do you do what you do?

2. Who shapes your life?

3. What do you do today that began because you wanted to identify with someone years ago?

4. In what ways did the people on your list shape your life? In what way are you allowing Jesus Christ to shape your life if you belong to Him?

It's true for everyone, isn't it? I hope you'll continue the discussion about identity in your family time this week by asking the questions above.

WHO SHAPES(D) YOUR LIFE?

When you think about the list of people or groups with whom you wished to identify and consider what you desired to gain from them, what affect did they have on your life? Like Eric, were you introduced to people who were bad influences and introduced you to destructive attitudes, activities, and habit patterns? Do you still participate in some of those activities today without realizing where the root lies?

Before going to the personal application for this week, take a moment and write down what thoughts or questions have come to mind as you have read your assignment.

_____

_____

_____

_____

Before you attend your small group meeting, lead your family in the following exercises. Take notes of what was shared so you can share it with the group.

PERSONAL APPLICATION

1. In the first lesson, you made a list of the people and groups with whom you wanted to connect when you were between the ages of 14-16 and presently. Now take those same names and ask yourself, "What did I do to gain the connection with them?" What habits began, what words did you adopt, or what changed about your life? Write your answer in the right column below. After you have done this exercise, lead your family to do the same.

Identity source (14-16)   **How did they shape your life?**

_____   _____

_____   _____

_____   _____

_____   _____

_____   _____

Identity source (now)   **How did they shape your life?**

_____   _____

_____   _____

_____   _____

_____   _____

_____   _____

2. It is also helpful to look at this principle from your own perspective. There are people in your lives who have sought to be associated or identified with you because you are a blessing to them. Below, note the changes in their lives because they have connected with you in the left column and the blessing you are to them in the right column.

Who is identifying with you?　　**What changes do you observe?**

_____　　_____

_____　　_____

_____　　_____

_____　　_____

_____　　_____

_____　　_____

PERSONAL PRAYER INVITATION

What have you learned about yourself in this lesson? Ask the Holy Spirit to speak to your heart. Ask Him what He sees in light of the verses above. Write down what comes to mind.

_____

_____

_____

Interact with Jesus on a personal level. When you allow someone other than God to shape your life, what do you think He thinks about it? Have you considered that perhaps the spiritual power of a bad habit with which you are still struggling may be rooted in your having never repented of looking to someone other than God to shape your life and to be the source of your identity? Have you ever expressed your repentance and sorrow for having hardened your heart in order to worship a creature instead of the Creator? How did it damage your witness for Christ or glory to God?

I encourage you to take as much time as is necessary to clear your conscience and ask the Holy Spirit to set you free from anything that still binds you as a result of identifying with those who were not believers. I hope by now you have memorized the daily declaration. This week, use it as a starting point and let the Holy Spirit broaden and deepen your praise and worship of Jesus Christ.

- I belong to Jesus.

- His Spirit lives within me and is my source of power.

- His Spirit will change me as He fills and lives in me.

- I am blessed to be God's son.

- I will consider my old self as having died and will be alive to what the life of God in me loves and hates.

- Father, please give me the fullness of the Holy Spirit as you promised through Jesus Christ for your glory.

SCRIPTURE MEMORY

Choose two or more scriptures to memorize this week.

Matthew 16:17-18 And Jesus said to him, "Blessed are you, Simon Barjona, because flesh and blood did not reveal this to you, but My Father who is in heaven. I also say to you that you are Peter, and upon this rock I will build My church; and the gates of Hades will not overpower it."

John 5:30 "I can do nothing on My own initiative. As I hear, I judge; and My judgment is just, because I do not seek My own will, but the will of Him who sent Me."

John 8:28 So Jesus said, "When you lift up the Son of Man, then you will know that I am He, and I do nothing on My own initiative, but I speak these things as the Father taught Me."

John 10:30 "I and the Father are one."

John 12:49 "For I did not speak on My own initiative, but the Father Himself who sent Me has given Me a commandment as to what to say and what to speak."

John 14:9-10 Jesus said to him, "Have I been so long with you, and yet you have not come to know Me, Philip? He who has seen Me has seen the Father; how can you say, 'Show us the Father'? Do you not believe that I am in the Father, and the Father is in Me? The words that I say to you I do not speak on My own initiative, but the Father abiding in Me does His works."

John 16:13 "*But when He, the Spirit of truth, comes, He will guide you into all the truth; for He will not speak on His own initiative, but whatever He hears, He will speak; and He will disclose to you what is to come.*"

GROUP INTERACTION

1. Begin with prayer, acknowledging the identity truths you've been declaring each morning and the power God offers to you as you meet.

2. Each member of the group quote the two verses memorized and share what was meaningful about them.

3. Share what thoughts or questions you had after reading the assignment.

4. Share about your personal application on Identity Principle Three.

5. How is identifying with this small group shaping your life?

6. Close with prayer for one another and for God's guidance as you study Lesson 6.

Lesson 6

IDENTITY PRINCIPLE THREE IN CHRIST

When we as believers in Jesus Christ think about who shapes our lives now, we certainly place Jesus at the top of the list. How does our identity with Jesus Christ impact our lives? Jesus' call to discipleship and eternal life is primarily a call to identify with Him. The Gospel of Mark records the following:

> *Mark 8:34 And He summoned the crowd with His disciples, and said to them, "If anyone wishes to come after Me, he must deny himself, and take up his cross and follow Me.*

> *Mark 8:35 For whoever wishes to save his life will lose it, but whoever loses his life for My sake and the gospel's will save it.*

> *Mark 8:36 For what does it profit a man to gain the whole world, and forfeit his soul?*

> *Mark 8:37 For what will a man give in exchange for his soul?*

> *Mark 8:38 For whoever is ashamed of Me and My words in this adulterous and sinful generation, the Son of Man will also be ashamed of him when He comes in the glory of His Father with the holy angels."*

Those who are ashamed of identifying with Jesus will find that He is ashamed of them when He returns in His glory. To put it in a positive light, Jesus was saying that when He returns in His glory, He will be unashamed and excited about those who are unashamed and excited about Him now. How do we express that we are not ashamed of Him now? We purposefully seek to identify with Him so we may be conformed to His image in every area of our lives.

IDENTITY PRINCIPLE THREE IN CHRIST: THE HOLY SPIRIT TRANSFORMS US INTO THE IMAGE OF JESUS CHRIST

Do you want to be identified with Jesus when He returns? That's quite a question, isn't it? It gives our lives an eternal perspective. Before going to the cross on our behalf, Jesus gave some wonderful news to His disciples. He was not going to leave them alone, but was going to come to them and fill them in the person of the Holy Spirit (John 14:16-20). This promise is just as real to us as it was to them. Ever since the first Pentecost when Jesus fulfilled His promise, the Holy Spirit has come into the lives of God's people from every tribe, tongue, and nation. The Holy Spirit's presence *is the presence of the risen Jesus Christ*.

We have studied earlier about the Holy Spirit as the power of God in those who belong to Jesus. Now we are considering His role as the sanctifier, transformer, and shaper of our lives—the experience of Identity Principle Three in our relationship with God. According to 2 Corinthians 3:18, the goal of His transforming work is the image of Jesus Christ. Born-again believers have the life of God in them, the Spirit of Christ, teaching, guiding, and living in them. It is He who makes the Word of God alive and purifying in their hearts enabling them to participate in His intercession and be transformed by the renewing of their minds.

THE HOLY SPIRIT TRANSFORMS US THROUGH THE SCRIPTURES

Like you learned the vocabulary and opinions of one with whom you wished to connect, so you search the Scriptures to learn the mind of Christ and His vocabulary. To identify with Jesus is to "let the word of Christ richly dwell within you (Col. 3:16). That's how He shapes your life. The Scriptures are sufficient for every need in life, teaching you how to think and how to act (2 Timothy 3:16). About the man who hears and acts on His words, Jesus said he was building on a firm foundation able to withstand the greatest storm of life, the judgment of God (Matthew 7:24-25). Jesus referred to those who hear His words and do them as His mother and brothers (Luke 8:21). Reading, learning, memorizing, meditating, and acting on God's Word is vital for our lives to be shaped into the image of Jesus Christ.

Answered prayer is a response to requests according to His Word abiding in His children, shaping their intercession (John 15:7). The Apostle Paul refers to the Word of God as the sword of the Spirit (Ephesians 6:17-18). Without a thorough knowledge of God's Word, our prayers will be selfish and powerless instead of aligned with His will and thus powerful. The Apostle James warned against asking with wrong motives of selfish pleasure (James 4:3). When the Holy Spirit brings God's Word to mind as we pray, faith is generated and we're transformed through personal encounters with the living Lord Jesus (Romans 10:17).

Spirit-filled worship, praise, and thanksgiving are based on God's Word. As we read or meditate on what is revealed in His Word, our souls respond much like when we overlook a grand and beautiful panorama in nature. The glory of the object elicits first awe and then a declaration of wonder.

The Holy Spirit transforms us through faith with obedience

If you are identifying with Jesus Christ, you wish to be like Him. The Spirit-empowered Word of God produces faith in our hearts from beginning to the end of our earthly experience with Christ. Peter expresses the alpha faith in Acts 15:8-9. "And God, who knows the heart, testified to them giving them the Holy Spirit, just as He also did to us; and He made no distinction between us and them, cleansing their hearts by faith." Then in his first epistle, speaking of those who have been born again by a living hope, he declared they are "protected by the power of God through faith for a salvation ready to be revealed in the last time" (1 Peter 1:5).

This faith is, of course, an active faith that produces obedience as illustrated in verse 2, as Peter describes the work of the Holy Spirit in those who have been chosen, "according to the foreknowledge of God the Father, by the sanctifying work of the Spirit, to obey Jesus Christ." Jesus, Paul, and John taught about the correlation between faith, love, and obedience. God-wrought faith works through love (Galatians 5:6). Spirit-born love produces obedience (John 14:21). As this process works in God's children, they are transformed, shaped into the likeness of Christ. Take a moment and give Him praise and thanksgiving for such mercy and grace!

Believers work out what God works in

What is the believer's part in this process of sanctification? We work out what God has worked in. Paul wrote to the Philippians, "So then, my beloved, just as you have always obeyed, not as in my presence only, but now much more in my absence, work out your salvation with fear and trembling; for it is God who is at work in you, both to will and to work for His good pleasure" (Phil. 2:12-13). John confidently asserts, "And everyone who has this hope fixed on Him purifies himself, just as He is pure" (1 John 3:3).

Although God is sovereign in all the affairs of man, the Scriptures also clearly explain the responsibility God's children have to conform themselves to the image of Christ. Their confidence isn't in their ability, but in God's goodness and grace. They know that God gives to His children what His law requires and thus it may be expected that they will seek to imitate Jesus because they are identified with Him just like they allowed their peers to shape their lives before they met Christ.

The author of Hebrews wrote something we should all remember. "Remember those who led you, who spoke the word of God to you; and considering the result of their conduct, imitate their faith" (Hebrews 13:7). And the Apostle John encouraged us with, "Beloved, do not imitate what is evil, but what is good. The one who does good is of God; the one who does evil has not seen God" (3 John 11). We also are shaped by the lives of others who are identifying with Jesus as we imitate their good example.

LIFE EXAMPLE

Before **Jim** became a Christian, he was known around his work as an angry slave-driver. His work associates didn't want to be around him. Jim developed a tough exterior and demeanor by watching his boss, his mentor in business. When first employed, Jim's supervisor rewarded task-oriented, no-nonsense, hard-hitting leadership. There was very little sensitivity or attention to relationship building. His boss, and thus Jim, considered it a weakness to allow relationships to get in the way of progress and production.

Jim was successful in business, but emotionally and spiritually he was empty. When a new employee, Larry, came into the office, Jim noticed something different about him immediately. He didn't laugh at the crude and dirty jokes or go drinking with the men after work. Larry was joyful most of the time, worked hard, and was patient with Jim's cold, hard demeanor. After a few weeks, Jim asked Larry why he didn't go out with the men when it was expected if he wanted to go further in the company. As Larry shared about his faith in Christ because of God's love revealed in the gospel and his love for his family, something happened in Jim's heart. He wanted what Larry had! After numerous conversations, Jim began to read the Bible Larry gave him and not long after that was born again by the Holy Spirit.

Jim was excited about forgiveness, a new eternal hope, and his new-found relationship with Christ and Larry. Almost immediately, he realized something had to change at work in his relationships. What would people think of Jesus if he continued to yell at them and make unreasonable demands? His love for

Jesus compelled him to reform his relational style. He also watched Larry's patience and tried to imitate him. Living with Jesus was a completely new way of living! As Jim learned about the importance of living out the gospel toward his wife and children, his marriage was saved and his relationships at home became fulfilling. Within a few months everyone in his family had come to know the Savior. He found he no longer wanted to trade two hours each evening with his family to be with the guys in the gym, bar, or restaurant like he used to.

Jim's relationship with Jesus impacted every area of his life. That's how it is with Jesus! Once Jim wanted to be identified with Christ more than anyone else, the process of transformation began. The more He learned from God's Word, Larry, fellow believers, and from fellowship with the Holy Spirit, the more his life changed at work, home, and in private. Jim's testimony is a great example of Identity Principle Three.

Meredith's story is very similar to Jim's. Her brother and sister-in-law had been praying for ten years that she would trust in Christ. Their witnessing efforts were met with repeated resistance. Meredith had a pre-school age daughter and was concerned about sending her to the public school because of the negative environment she knew was there. So when invited to a home education conference, Meredith was intrigued and attended with her brother and sister-in-law. At the conference, as the speaker shared the gospel and how God has provided a blueprint for family, her heart opened to Christ and she was born again.

Her life changed drastically. She resigned her job, dedicated herself to teaching her child at home, and began growing in her relationship with Jesus. Meredith was challenged and encouraged by her newfound relationships that accompanied her new life with Jesus. Whereas previously her life was shaped by her culture, it was now impacted by Jesus and dozens of families in her church.

PERSONAL APPLICATION

1. What thoughts and questions have entered your mind as you read this assignment?

_____

_____

_____

_____

2. When you were born again, what changes did you make in your lifestyle?

_____

_____

_____

_____

3. Write down the names of some people whose walk with Jesus you have imitated.

_____

_____

_____

4. Write down the names of some people who are imitating your walk with Jesus.

_____

_____

_____

5. Are there areas of life where you know you need to obey Jesus, but haven't had the courage? List those areas and ask Jesus to work in you.

_____

_____

_____

PERSONAL PRAYER INVITATION

The Laodicean church received a wonderful invitation from the Lord Jesus to enter into deeper fellowship and communion with Him. Read Revelation 3:14-22 and allow the Holy Spirit to lead you in prayer and fellowship with the Lord. Note below what comes to mind and be prepared to share about your experience in the group meeting.

_____

_____

_____

Scripture Memory

Choose two or more scriptures to memorize this week.

Mark 8:34 And He summoned the crowd with His disciples, and said to them, "If anyone wishes to come after Me, he must deny himself, and take up his cross and follow Me.

Mark 8:35 For whoever wishes to save his life will lose it, but whoever loses his life for My sake and the gospel's will save it.

Mark 8:36 For what does it profit a man to gain the whole world, and forfeit his soul?

Mark 8:37 For what will a man give in exchange for his soul?

Mark 8:38 For whoever is ashamed of Me and My words in this adulterous and sinful generation, the Son of Man will also be ashamed of him when He comes in the glory of His Father with the holy angels."

Rom. 6:4 Therefore we have been buried with Him through baptism into death, so that as Christ was raised from the dead through the glory of the Father, so we too might walk in newness of life.

Rom. 6:8 Now if we have died with Christ, we believe that we shall also live with Him,

Rom. 6:12-13 Therefore do not let sin reign in your mortal body so that you obey its lusts, and do not go on presenting the members of your body to sin as instruments of unrighteousness; but present yourselves to God as those alive from the dead, and your members as instruments of righteousness to God.

Rom 8:13-14 For if you are living according to the flesh, you must die; but if by the Spirit you are putting to death the deeds of the body, you will live. For all who are being led by the Spirit of God, these are sons of God.

2 Cor. 3:18 But we all, with unveiled face, beholding as in a mirror the glory of the Lord, are being transformed into the same image from glory to glory, just as from the Lord, the Spirit.

2 Cor. 13:5 Test yourselves to see if you are in the faith; examine yourselves! Or do you not recognize this about yourselves, that Jesus Christ is in you—unless indeed you fail the test?

GROUP INTERACTION

1. Share what you experienced in your personal prayer time this past week.

2. Discuss with the group what changes you made when you were first born-again.

3. Share the names of people who have been an encouragement to you in your walk with Jesus. What is it about them that you wish to imitate?

4. Share the names of people who are imitating your walk with Jesus.

5. Share the areas of life where you need to obey Jesus.

6. Close with prayer.

    a. For those who are imitating you.

    b. For each other for grace and courage to obey in the areas mentioned.

    c. With thanksgiving for God's grace and His power to transform you into His image.

Lesson 7

IDENTITY PRINCIPLE FOUR

FATHERS DIRECT THE IDENTITY COURSE OF THEIR CHILDREN BY WHAT THEY DO OR DON'T DO

Fathers for generations shape our lives in ways we don't realize. All of us have become taught by successive generations of fathers who have shaped our lives by what they did or didn't do. This goes all the way back to our first father, Adam! When he sinned, sin entered into the world and has infected every generation since (Rom. 5:12). The culture in which you live and have your identity bears the affects of the curse and its accompanying iniquities.

Fathers determined the philosophies of life, religions, work habits, and family patterns of every nation—its culture. I'm not ignoring the impact of women, but their place in each culture is determined by what the men did or didn't do. In order to be identified with your people and have the power of their acceptance, your fathers (the men in your society) and you have allowed the culture to shape your lives. The only exception to this is when someone desires to identify with another father, people, or culture. Isn't this true?

ABSENT FATHERS CREATE EMPTY CHILDREN

If you look back to the previous identity exercises at the list of people with whom you wished to identify, you might conclude that you gave those people the power to shape your life. In one sense, you did open the door to their influence. However, you might be surprised to discover that it was your father or the lack of having a father that was the primary cause. Your father, by what he did or didn't do, impacted your search for identity. If a father doesn't fill his children with his presence, love, and purpose, then they will be searching for someone or something to fill the void. Absent fathers create empty children and rear another generation unprepared for life, both practically and spiritually.

THE FATHER DIRECTS THE IDENTITY COURSE OF HIS CHILDREN

A father actively or passively establishes his child's identity course. First, we see this principle explicitly stated by Simon in his declaration of Jesus' identity in Matthew 16:16. Jesus' identity is directly related to His Father. "Simon Peter answered, 'You are the Christ, the Son of the living God.'" The Father directing Jesus' course in life is affirmed as we read that Jesus never did or spoke anything on His own initiative (John 5:30; 8:28, 42; 12:49; 14:10). He lived by every word that proceeded out of the mouth of His Father (Matt. 4:4).

Second, this principle is implied in Jesus' reply to Simon in Matthew 16:17-18. He told Simon his understanding of Jesus' identity came from a revelation from His Father in heaven thus testifying to his belonging to His Father. This called for a new identity: Simon became Peter.

> *And Jesus said to him, "Blessed are you, Simon Barjona, because flesh and blood did not reveal this to you, but My Father who is in heaven. I also say to you that you are Peter, and upon this rock I will build My church; and the gates of Hades will not overpower it."*

Third, in a spiritual sense, this principle is verified in the application of the gospel. Everyone who is born again receives the Holy Spirit, the Spirit of the Son, because each belongs to the Father (Galatians 4:7). Our hearts turn to God, the Father, because His heart is turned to us! He thus directs our identity in life through His Spirit, who seals, directs, and protects us (Ephesians 1:13-14).

Fourth, this principle is evident in life through various cultural rituals and examples. Children are typically identified by the names of their fathers. In many cultures, the last names actually communicate sonship/sonhood. For instance, *ovich* in Russian means son of. In Scandinavian countries *sson* or *ssen* indicates one is a son of a man (Andersson). In English, John's son was at one time identified as Johnson. Believers are called sons of God, when identified by God (1 John 3:1).

Some groups, such as those of the Jewish faith, have ceremonies celebrating the identification of sons and daughters with their fathers' faith and identity. Some tribes in Africa continue centuries old rituals of fathers "calling out" the sons of the community into manhood.

Fifth, this principle can be observed in our society. If a father doesn't fill his son or daughter with his spirit (his influence) providing hope for the future and a meaningful or purposeful relationship, the son or daughter experiences a nagging emptiness. This emptiness demands to be filled. It is a longing to belong or be connected to power. The children whose father doesn't have time for them or who doesn't know how to provide a relationship with hope for the future will seek relationships or experiences offering what they lack.

If you've ever coached children or youth you have probably noticed the boys or girls who are lacking direction and love from their fathers. They are starving for attention and approval! Gangs become surrogate fathers to sons abandoned by derelict dads. The popular tenth grade cheerleader sets the dress fads for dozens of girls who want to be connected with her because she gets the attention of the boys. Her power becomes their power. But why would the girls want the attention of the boys? Why does a guy want to join a gang? One primary reason is because dads haven't known the importance of sealing their sons and daughters in their identity and thus leave them open, empty, and vulnerable.

On the positive side, exemplifying the relationship between the heavenly Father and His Son, Jesus, a father may direct the identity course of his son or daughter by what he does. If a father has a vision for developing and maintaining a relationship with his children which prepares them for life, fills their emotional and spiritual tanks, and provides clear hope for their futures, he sets them on a course of fullness and purpose.

FATHERS MUST SEAL THEIR CHILDREN'S IDENTITIES

Imagine going into a store to purchase a bottle of water. Upon finding one, you check the cap and notice the seal is broken. Would you purchase that bottle? Probably not, because you fear someone may have put a contaminant into the water, or perhaps someone has actually taken a swig from it! We seal bottles to protect the contents and to preserve what is contained therein. The seal is an assurance.

Now think of your children as bottles and your giving meaning, purpose, and hope to them as sealing them. That seal protects all of the truth and teaching you put into them and prevents their being polluted by lies, worldly philosophies, and carnal allurements. However, if you don't seal them, in effect you send them off to school open, without sealed caps. What you've instilled in them may be lost, and their souls may become open seedbeds for anything promising them a sense of significance and power. The ignorant or otherwise occupied father determines the identity course of his child by not sealing his child.

ONE FATHER'S EXAMPLE

One father did it this way. On his son's 12th birthday, in an official and loving way, he communicated to his son that he belonged to him, was loved by him, and together they were going to walk from boyhood into manhood. Here are some of the ideas this father had for sealing a son.

- Give an official acknowledgement of belonging/connection.

- Give vision and meaning for the relationship.

- Teach him about his body.

- Teach him how to be a leader.

- Teach him how to know God's Word, pray, interpret Scripture, and discern truth from error.

- Teach him how to understand a woman and love her with God's kind of love.

- Teach him skills men need to care for a family.

- Covenant to walk through life together.

- Assist him in discerning God's will for his life's work, ministry, and mate.

- Inform him as he becomes secure in his identity in Christ, he will decrease and the Heavenly Father will increase.

- You may learn more at www.spiritofelijah.com/chariot/chariot_39.php.

Obviously this was the beginning of a long process that took place daily. The important thing to note is the hope communicated to the son. Meaning, purpose, vision, hope, and relationship were communicated. This father's heart was turned to his son, and the result was the son's heart turning toward the father. This sealed the son; much like the Holy Spirit seals the sons of God, and a cap seals a bottle. Without this process, a son may seek other identity sources in women, careers, and money.

HOW ABOUT YOU AND YOUR FATHER?

I've recommended you make a list of the people with whom you wished to connect, the power or treasure they offered to you, which was appealing, and how those relationships shaped your life. Would your life be different today if your father had done with you what the father above did? If your father did or didn't seal you and lead you to your identity in Christ, why did he or didn't he?

The answer lies with his father—either his earthly father or his spiritual father. If you think of your father as a son of his father, you may realize his father didn't know to seal him or teach him about these identity principles. When he became your father he didn't know what to do. It wasn't that he didn't love you, he just didn't know. He did the best he could with what he had. Perhaps he was still searching for his identity when you came along and therefore, he left you to do the same.

Many men need to release their dads and forgive them. For years they have held bitterness and unforgiveness in their hearts due to abandonment, neglect, and hurt. In an effort to fill the void in their souls, they made foolish decisions as they sought to identify with people who ultimately couldn't fill the emptiness and in many cases led them into destructive ways. These people became idols of the heart and have taken their hearts away from God, the Father, Jesus Christ, and relationship with the Holy Spirit. Is this your experience? Will you forgive your father and mother for not sealing you?

How are your children going to withstand the current of evil in their schools, community, and flesh? The only way is to be firmly rooted in their identity with you and with Jesus Christ. We must send them out sealed and full. God's plan is that they learn these principles first with their earthly fathers and then transfer that truth to their heavenly Father. We'll learn more about that relationship next week.

WILL THE REAL MAN PLEASE STAND UP?

Men ordinarily have numerous identities: at work, home, and church. In order to connect with men at work, it's tempting to allow them to shape one's language, mannerisms, music, etc. Then at home, a man wants his wife to make him happy and comfortable, so he conforms to her values and standards in the home on many things. In some cases, for men to belong to their Christian wives, they discover it is necessary to belong to the church. So, in order to get a wife, they go to church and do whatever is required to belong. Perhaps they pray a prayer of invitation, learn the church-speak, and present an image of conservatism and religiosity.

God intends for our source of identity to be the same everywhere. Would the men at work discover you to be the same man at home? Would your wife and pastor find you to be the same man at work they know at home and church? If there is a difference, when did this pattern of split personality begin? Probably when you were a child or teen! In order to belong to your parents, you acted one way at home. However, to belong to your friends at school, you donned another set of standards in speech and conduct. You learned to live with the dichotomy and probably sought to keep the two worlds separate.

People haven't changed. You may find your teens doing the same thing without realizing why. They may be reluctant to have their friends come to the house if they have two identities. You may experience a resistance when you try to enter their world at some point. Perhaps they are afraid you will discover they aren't who they want you to think they are.

IT'S A MATTER OF THE HEART

The important thing to remember is that our hearts follow after our treasures. Our treasures are revealed in whom we want to identify or connect with. God's Word commands us to love Him with all of our hearts. It's the key to our identity and fulfillment.

Who has the heart of your child? The one who fills him or her with a reason to connect and identify. As a parent and forerunner for the Lord, your challenge is to first provide a rich example of someone who is identified and filled with the Spirit of Christ. Second, you fill the soul of your child with your spirit (your influence, and that doesn't mean bullying), which will seal their hearts. Teach them these principles. Help them work with the principles so they can understand themselves and those around them. And most importantly, lead them to identify with God, the Father, through a relationship with Jesus Christ. The purpose of the *Walking Worthy Series* is to provide God's truth and personal encounters with Him to you may be filled with His Spirit in order for you to fulfill your ministry to the next generation.

PERSONAL APPLICATION

1.   Write down your thoughts and questions. Perhaps you might summarize what you've read in a few short sentences.

_____

_____

_____

_____

2.   As you look at your lifestyle—your values, time management, financial stewardship, marriage, child-training and education, and relationships—how does it compare with the lifestyle of the majority of people in your culture?

Are your children different in vision and values from their peers? Sometimes we get caught in the culture current and fail to think about what we are doing and why we are doing it. This exercise is designed to encourage you to think about how you are like your fathers and your generation.

Area of Life	My Culture's Way	My Earthly Father's Way	My Way
Time management			
Financial stewardship			
Marriage relationship			
Your role in family			
Discipline of children			
Education of children			
Relationship with children			
Moral purity			

PERSONAL PRAYER INVITATION

1.   Express thanksgiving to God for the blessings He gave through your father. It's important that you acknowledge God's sovereignty over all relationships, especially those established by Him. Being a child of your father is a *calling* from God.

2.   If you find your heart cold or embittered toward your parents, why not be done with it! If their parents didn't know how to prepare their children for their callings in life, then they need your forgiveness and mercy—just like you need forgiveness and mercy from your children. For the glory of God, your health, and freedom, release your parents from your judgment and pray for them. (If they have passed away, then ask the Lord to release you from the stronghold of unforgiveness and bitterness.) Thank Him for the cross!

SCRIPTURE MEMORY

Choose two or more scriptures to memorize this week.

> *Rom. 5:12* *Therefore, just as through one man sin entered into the world, and death through sin, and so death spread to all men, because all sinned—*

> *2 Kings 17:38-41* *"The covenant that I have made with you, you shall not forget, nor shall you fear other gods. But the LORD your God you shall fear; and He will deliver you from the hand of all your enemies." However, they did not listen, but they did according to their earlier custom. So while these nations feared the LORD, they also served their idols; their children likewise and their grandchildren, as their fathers did, so they do to this day.*

> *Deuteronomy 6:1-2, 7* *"Now this is the commandment, the statutes and the judgments which the LORD your God has commanded me to teach you, that you might do them in the land where you are going over to possess it, so that you and your son and your grandson might fear the LORD your God, to keep all His statutes and His commandments which I command you, all the days of your life, and that your days may be prolonged.... You shall teach them diligently to your sons and shall talk of them when you sit in your house and when you walk by the way and when you lie down and when you rise up."*

> *Jer. 3:25* *"Let us lie down in our shame, and let our humiliation cover us; for we have sinned against the LORD our God, we and our fathers, from our youth even to this day. And we have not obeyed the voice of*

the LORD our God."

Jer. 6:21 Therefore, thus says the LORD, "Behold, I am laying stumbling blocks before this people and they will stumble against them, fathers and sons together; neighbor and friend will perish."

Jer. 9:14 "But have walked after the stubbornness of their heart and after the Baals, as their fathers taught them..."

GROUP INTERACTION

1. Share what you experienced in your personal prayer time this past week.

2. Quote the verses you memorized and share why they were meaningful.

3. Discuss what you learned from your reading assignment.

4. Share your observations about the comparisons of your lifestyle with your culture's way and your father's way.

5. Close with prayer.

Lesson 8

IDENTITY PRINCIPLE FOUR IN CHRIST

THE HEAVENLY FATHER DIRECTS THE IDENTITY COURSE OF HIS SONS THROUGH A RELATIONSHIP WITH HIS SON, JESUS CHRIST

To the degree that your fathers identified with the God of the universe, the Father of Jesus Christ, and honored His revelation (the Bible), your culture will be righteous. In contrast, to the degree your fathers identified with the god of this world (Satan) and honored his empty philosophies, your culture will be unrighteous. The differences between the two fathers (God and Satan) and the two cultures (righteous and unrighteous) have always produced conflict and forced an ultimate decision—you can't be friends with both because *both* are masters. Jesus taught in the Sermon on the Mount that no man can serve two masters (Matthew 6:24). The Apostle James emphasized this point in his letter, "You adulteresses, do you not know that friendship with the world is hostility toward God? Therefore whoever wishes to be a friend of the world makes himself an enemy of God" (James 4:4).

This spiritual conflict gives insight into Jesus' calling to His disciples. "If anyone comes to Me, and does not hate his own father and mother and wife and children and brothers and sisters, yes, and even his own life, he cannot be My disciple" (Luke 14:26). Some have wrongly concluded that Jesus was calling those in ministry to forsake their families and invest their lives 100 percent in the ministry. Since other passages clearly *command* husbands to love their wives (Eph. 5:25-33) and teach and discipline their children (Deut. 6:7-9; Eph. 6:4), such an interpretation must be dismissed.

What was Jesus saying? In affect, Jesus called the sons and daughters of

God to identify with His Father and with Him to the sacrifice of their identity with their national culture. It is a heart issue. Jesus must be Lord of all relationships in life. This call to discipleship hasn't changed. The radical nature of Jesus' call is the same today as it was 2000 years ago! However, there is a difference between the *call* to follow Jesus that goes out to everyone in the world and the *calling* of God, the Father, through the powerful work of the Holy Spirit.

TRUE BELIEVERS ARE SONS OF GOD AND ARE HIS WORKMANSHIP

God, the Father, establishes a believer's identity as He works in his or her heart by the power of His Spirit. Remember the fourth identity principle: our identity is determined by what our father does or doesn't do. The Apostle Paul taught the Galatians that the presence and work of the Holy Spirit is proof-positive they belong to Him and He is their father. "Because you are sons, God has sent forth the Spirit of His Son into our hearts, crying, "Abba! Father!" (Galatians 4:6). He encouraged the Corinthians about God's work in them. "But by His doing you are in Christ Jesus" (1 Corinthians 1:30). The beloved Apostle John rejoiced, "See, how great a love the Father has bestowed on us, that we would be called children of God; and such we are" (1 John 3:1).

> *"But God, being rich in mercy, because of His great love with which He loved us, even when we were dead in our transgressions, made us alive together with Christ (by grace you have been saved), and raised us up with Him, and seated us with Him in the heavenly places in Christ Jesus, so that in the ages to come He might show the surpassing riches of His grace in kindness toward us in Christ Jesus. For by grace you have been saved through faith; and that not of yourselves, it is the gift of God; not as a result of works, so that no one may boast. For we are His workmanship, created in Christ Jesus for good works, which God prepared beforehand so that we would walk in them" (Ephesians 2:4-10).*

Notice the emphasis in the passage above, as well as the one following, is on the work of our Father. Our identity with Christ is established by God. "By God's doing are you in Christ Jesus..." (1 Corinthians 1:30a).

GOD, THE FATHER, ADOPTED US THROUGH JESUS CHRIST

> *"Grace to you and peace from God our Father and the Lord Jesus Christ. Blessed be the God and Father of our Lord Jesus Christ, who has blessed us with every spiritual blessing in the heavenly places in Christ, just as He chose us in Him before the foundation of the world, that we*

would be holy and blameless before Him. In love He predestined us to adoption as sons through Jesus Christ to Himself, according to the kind intention of His will, to the praise of the glory of His grace, which He freely bestowed on us in the Beloved. In Him we have redemption through His blood, the forgiveness of our trespasses, according to the riches of His grace which He lavished on us" (Ephesians 1:2-8).

In Christ, we have been received into God's family!

GOD SEALS HIS CHILDREN

The gospel provides insight into this process of sealing a child. The heavenly Father seals His children and we can learn from His example. If His children need sealing, then our children also need sealing. Let's first look at some verses of Scripture.

2 Cor. 1:22 Who also sealed us and gave us the Spirit in our hearts as a pledge.

Eph. 1:13 In Him, you also, after listening to the message of truth, the gospel of your salvation—having also believed, you were sealed in Him with the Holy Spirit of promise.

Eph. 4:30 Do not grieve the Holy Spirit of God, by whom you were sealed for the day of redemption.

The sealing of the Spirit has a purpose: to secure and protect the saints for the day of redemption—our future hope. The Holy Spirit is the influence of the Father and the Son. He was given to us so we might know both the Father and the Son and thus experience eternal life (John 14:16-21; 17:3). He guides us (John 16:13), helps us (John 14:16), comforts us (2 Corinthians 1:4), teaches us (John 14:26), convicts us of sin, righteousness, and judgment (John 16:8-11), and fills us with the presence of Christ (John 14:17-21). From the Holy Spirit's ministry, we can learn how to seal our own children.

THE FATHER'S HEART TURNED TO HIS SONS TURNS THEIR HEARTS TO HIM

If God had not loved us first, the Apostle John says we would never have loved Him (1 John 4:19). Luke recorded the Holy Spirit's application of this fourth identity principle when He spoke to Zacharias regarding his new son, John, later to be called "the Baptist." When fathers' hearts are turned to their sons, the sons' hearts are prepared for the Lord (Luke 1:17). When the heavenly Father's heart turns to His children, He does something. He sends His Spirit to them and their hearts turn away from identifying with the world and turn to Him! The Holy Spirit described this work as the Spirit and power of Elijah. This work of the Spirit of the Father prepares the heart for a relationship with Jesus Christ.

IDENTITY QUESTIONS

To Whom Do You Belong?

Who is Your Power Source?

Who Shapes Your Life?

Who is Your Father and What Has He Done?

The answers to the above four questions describe your identity. If you have the Holy Spirit in you, then God is your father. You belong to Him. He is your power source. He shapes your life. Being sons and daughters of the father of Jesus Christ should be the defining relationship and power in your life. Believers should be "peculiar" to their neighbors, work associates, and friends, who are living to identify with their culture. Certainly there are some similarities, however, if they are in step with the mainstream of the nations surrounding them, what hope and good news do they have to share? Apart from their public profession and church attendance, what distinguishes them from everyone else? God's children are to be a people of vision and light with a generational mindset because our Father has revealed His vision for us in every area of life. The Father makes the difference!

Have you realized what the heavenly Father has done or offers to you? He is the power, meaning, fullness, and life your heart has been looking for! All is found in Jesus Christ. In belonging to Christ, we belong to God, the Father. His ministry—our identification with Him—should supercede our identifying with anyone and everything else in this world. He is our father, His power is our hope, and it is He who should shape our lives by filling us with His Spirit.

You will find the world's pull on you is directly related to the spiritual reality of your identification with God as your Father and the sealing of His Spirit. When you ignore or fail to apply the truth of your connection with your heavenly Father (if indeed you have one), your power to resist temptation decreases. Temptation uses emptiness as an ally. On the contrary, when you are filled with who you are in Christ, you find inner strength to resist and stand against the onslaught from the world.

PERSONAL APPLICATION

1. Make a note of what came to mind as you read the lesson. Do you have any questions?

_____

_____

_____

_____

2. Contrast the church culture from what God's Word says about each area of life. Ideally they should be the same, however, that is not always the case. What Scriptures come to mind for each area of life? Write them under "God's Way."

Area of Life	My Church's Way	God's Way
Time management		
Financial stewardship		
Marriage relationship		
Your role in family		

Discipline of children

Education of children

Relationship with children

Moral purity

3.   Describe your feelings about being radical to your culture (even church culture) or displeasing your Father in heaven?

_____

_____

_____

_____

4.   If you were to identify with Jesus and His Father, what do the Holy Spirit and God's Word indicate would have to change?

Area of Life   Changes I need to make to identify with my heavenly Father
Time management

Financial stewardship

Marriage relationship

Your role in family

Discipline of children

Education of children

Relationship with children

Moral purity

PERSONAL PRAYER INVITATION

If you have not begun a relationship with the heavenly Father, why wait? Go to Him now, in prayer. Confess your sin of identification with others. Receive His forgiveness on the basis of His placing your sin on His Son at the cross and ask Him for the gift of the Holy Spirit whom He promised to send after His resurrection to those who repent and believe that Jesus is God's Son. It's a matter of identity! Do you want to be connected to Jesus when He returns in the glory of His Father? If so, then listen to the words of the Father quoted by the Apostle Paul in 2 Corinthians 6:17-18.

"*I WILL DWELL IN THEM AND WALK AMONG THEM; AND I WILL BE THEIR GOD, AND THEY SHALL BE MY PEOPLE.* "Therefore, *COME OUT FROM THEIR MIDST AND*

BE SEPARATE," says the Lord. "AND DO NOT TOUCH WHAT IS UNCLEAN..."

"And I will welcome you. And I will be a father to you, and you shall be sons and daughters to Me," says the Lord Almighty.

The "unclean" refers to the idols of this world, the things to which people in the culture surrounding you look for happiness and power. Will you turn from those things and turn your heart fully to the Father and to His Son, Jesus Christ? You may do so, right now by humbling yourself before Him in prayer.

If you know you are a son of God, then continue to practice your identity confession this week. Ask Him for grace to make the changes needed in order to please your heavenly Father.

SCRIPTURE MEMORY

Choose two or more scriptures to memorize this week.

Luke 14:26 "If anyone comes to Me, and does not hate his own father and mother and wife and children and brothers and sisters, yes, and even his own life, he cannot be My disciple."

Galatians 4:6-7 Because you are sons, God has sent forth the Spirit of His Son into our hearts, crying, "Abba! Father!" Therefore you are no longer a slave, but a son; and if a son, then an heir through God.

Ephesians 2:4 But God, being rich in mercy, because of His great love with which He loved us,

Ephesians 2:5 even when we were dead in our transgressions, made us alive together with Christ (by grace you have been saved),

Ephesians 2:6 and raised us up with Him, and seated us with Him in the heavenly places in Christ Jesus,

Ephesians 2:7 so that in the ages to come He might show the surpassing riches of His grace in kindness toward us in Christ Jesus.

Ephesians 2:8 For by grace you have been saved through faith; and that not of yourselves, it is the gift of God;

Ephesians 2:9 not as a result of works, so that no one may boast.

Ephesians 2:10 For we are His workmanship, created in Christ Jesus for good works, which God prepared beforehand so that we would walk in them.

James 4:4 You adulteresses, do you not know that friendship with the world is hostility toward God? Therefore whoever wishes to be a friend of the world makes himself an enemy of God.

1 John 3:1 See how great a love the Father has bestowed on us, that we would be called children of God; and such we are. For this reason the world does not know us, because it did not know Him.

1 John 4:19 We love, because He first loved us.

GROUP INTERACTION

1. Share what you experienced in your personal prayer time this past week.

2. Quote the verses you memorized and share why they were meaningful to you.

3. Discuss what you learned about identifying with God as your heavenly Father.

4. Share what areas of life you know you need to change in order to please your heavenly Father and walk worthy of being identified as His son.

5. Close with prayer.

SUMMARY OF WALKING WORTHY AS A SON OF GOD

In Volume One you learned the following important truths:

- Identity has to do with to whom you want to belong or connect.

- I belong to Christ and His Spirit must fill and drive me so I live as an expression of that connection.

- Identity has to do with power.

- The Holy Spirit in me is my source of power.

- The source of power shapes one's life.

- The Holy Spirit transforms us into the image of Jesus Christ.

- Fathers direct the identity course of their children by what they do or don't do.

- The Heavenly Father directs the identity course of His children through a relationship with His Son, Jesus Christ.

Which one of the above was most meaningful to you?

THE WALKING WORTHY SERIES
A SERIES TO EQUIP MEN FOR LIFE AND ETERNITY

VOLUME ONE: WALKING WORTHY AS A SON OF GOD

VOLUME TWO: WALKING WORTHY AS A HUSBAND

Whether you are married or plan to be married, being equipped to walk worthy of your calling as a husband to your wife should be a top priority. It's one of the ways men can powerfully preach the gospel of Jesus' love for His bride. When a man loves his wife as Christ loves His church, he walks in a manner worthy of the Lord Jesus. Drawing from the well of wisdom revealed in Jesus Christ, you'll learn about and practice walking worthy of your calling as a husband.

VOLUME THREE: WALKING WORTHY AS A FATHER

There are few relationships in life more important than a father's relationship with his children. Walking worthy of your calling as a father explodes with meaning when we consider God's plan for fathers—to be forerunners to their children, leading them to know God the Father through His Son, Jesus Christ. In this series of lessons you'll see how you can reflect the love and care of the Heavenly Father to the next generation.

VOLUME FOUR: WALKING WORTHY AS A PROVIDER

Few areas of life are more challenging for men than balancing their work responsibilities with their family and ministry responsibilities. Walking worthy as a provider for your family requires knowledge of God's Word as well as a daily walk with the Holy Spirit. Practical biblical insights in this volume will encourage you in how to glorify God as He provides for ministry, family, and those in need through you.

VOLUME FIVE: WALKING WORTHY AS A MEMBER OF THE BODY OF CHRIST

Fulfilling your calling as a member of the body of Christ is an important aspect of walking worthy of your calling. What does it mean to be a member of Christ's body? Why is it important to understand one's gifts and roles in building up God's holy temple? Answers to these questions and more will be learned through this volume.

OTHER RESOURCES AVAILABLE FROM THE SPIRIT OF ELIJAH MINISTRIES

Equipping Men .... available on CD/DVD/MP3

Rising to the Call .... available on CD/DVD/MP3

Teenagers 101 .... available on CD/MP3

On Fire for the Gospel .... available on CD/MP3

Unshakable Faith .... available on CD/DVD/MP3

Marriage for God's Glory .... available on CD/DVD/MP3

Raised Up With Christ .... available on CD/DVD/MP3

Equipped to Love .... book by Norm Wakefield

Anchored in Christ .... book by Norm Wakefield

Walking Worthy Series for Women (coming 2009) .. book series by Norm Wakefield

Glorious Grace .... music CD or audio tape by Norm Wakefield

To order any of these resources or to find out more about them, please visit our website:

http://www.spiritofelijah.com

Or email us at: info@spiritofelijah.com